Hezekiah's Prayer

Lessons From a Man of Prayer

Thomas Murosky, Ph.D.

Kings of All Creation Series Vol 2

Our Walk In Christ Publishing
State College, PA

Published by Our Walk in Christ Publishing
State College, PA
www.owicpub.com

Hezekiah's Prayer: Approaching God in Humble Prayer

First Printing 2019
ISBN: 978-1-7325696-8-3 (sc)
ISBN: 978-1-7325696-9-0 (e)

The Internet addresses in this book are accurate at the time of publication. They are provided as a resource, but due to the nature of the Internet, those addresses may change.

Commitment to Open Source: Our Walk in Christ Publishing uses FOSS software where available. This book was produced with LibreOffice, GNU Image Manipulator Program, Sigil, and the following open fonts: Charis SIL, PlainBlack, and DejaVu Sans. Chapter dividers obtained from https://openclipart.org. Audiobook edition produced with Audacity and Kid3.

LCCN: 2019953601

Dedication

This book is dedicated to my mentor, David Hurd, who has taught me more about praying in difficult times than any other human agent. The way you seek God is an inspiration, and through your example I have also seen how God responds to prayer.

Acknowledgments

I wish to acknowledge my followers and readers in my online communities for the encouragement to continue writing and teaching across the spectrum of the Christian faith. Thanks for watching and reading. Please stay in touch!

I also wish to acknowledge my financial backers who have provided support allowing me to spend more time researching, learning, and writing on Christian topics. Without your support, I would not be able to release these books.

Thanks also to the beta readers for the initial thoughts on the manuscript before publication, the Christian Writers Roundtable in State College, and to Kate for doing the final round of editing.

Finally thanks to you, my readers, who make putting my thoughts on paper, digital ink, and audio tracks worth the while! I pray that my experiences while growing in my faith will help you grow as you walk in Christ.

Table of Contents

Introduction

Physical Chemistry is a type of hard I had never experienced in a college course before. By my junior year I earned the reputation as a person who could not be stopped by any academic challenge, and so when this impossible class hit my schedule I started out strong; full of sinful pride. I fought through the first exam with flying colors and even managed to get through the rest of the first semester without a hitch. I thought I was unstoppable, but I was not.

I realized by the third exam in the second semester that I had finally met my academic match! I was conquered, beaten down, destroyed by the Hamiltonian operator which so eluded me! My academic studies were finally failing me!

I locked myself into the dark basement section of my back office where I was able to get away. I cried out into the darkness at nothing, for at this time I did not know God. I was thinking this would be the first time I would fail a course in my college years. I exhausted every avenue for success I could think up on my own: studying more, buying extra books on the topic, doing more problems. I did everything...except go and talk to the professor. I decided finally to humble myself and knock on the office door to ask for help, and let's be honest, not a lot of people could help a confused student understand Physical Chemistry!

I use this story to illustrate how many of us behave when we encounter problems in life. In my little story, it was only when I showed up to the professor's office that I finally realize he was willing to help all along. It only took humbling myself enough to ask for assistance from the one source who could really help. And when problems come in our life, we need to humbly ask for help with the only source who truly understands and has power to help us: God of Heaven.

Like many people, I put off seeking the one person who could help me the most until the very last minute!

Why do we do this to ourselves? Because in the west, we are brought up to find our own solutions to our problems rather than seek those who can actually help us solve them. We are taught to be self-sufficient. It is certainly an American construct to be independent, to solve our own problems. Though often we are taught to employ advice from our trusted family and friends, God is the one source with the knowledge to best understand our struggles, and the power to help us through them.

It all boils down to independence versus interdependence. **Independence is when we try to be an island unto ourselves**; we attempt to be our own person, to be free from the counsel of one another. **Interdependence is when we recognize we cannot be entirely self-sufficient and we seek the help of others, and ultimately the help of God.** The Bible is clear we are not to be alone, but rather that we are built for community and fellowship. Before sin entered into the world, God placed the man, Adam, in the Garden of Eden to tend it, but He said, *It is not good for the man to be alone (Genesis 2:18)*. The woman was made for the man and the institution of marriage was created; a permanent fellowship for people on earth.

Outside of marriage, we also have friends. Remember King David and his best friend Jonathan (*1 Samuel 18:1-4*). They loved one another with a deep bond of friendship that is unparalleled in the rest of the Old Testament. After the time of Christ, however, a deep form of love and friendship was often spoken of in the various epistles. We are to love everyone without the expectation of return; the same *agape* love which Christ demonstrated when He died on the cross.

But these human friendships are not all we are to have. The greatest bond of fellowship happened when Jesus died on the cross and gave us all direct access to God through prayer. Our fellowship with Him is the ultimate relationship we can have, and like all relationships, communication is very important. Such communication with God is prayer.

Prayer is interdependence; the humble knowledge that we cannot solve all our problems on earth. We need to have communication to bear our soul and to ask for help, both of which are difficult for us to do because our society teaches us to never seek help. We may ask for prayer requests, but often the majority of us rarely take those requests directly to God first. Hezekiah learned early in his life to have fellowship with God through His Word, through the prophets, and most importantly, through Prayer. In this book, we will be learning about this king, where he came from, and how he became known as the most righteousness king since David. By the end of this book we will understand why God listened to this king when he took his concerns before God, and hopefully, we, too, will learn the importance of prayer and how to be heard by God.

1

Learning Objectives

Prayer is at once a simple task which a person new to Christ utters without deep understanding of what it really is or does, while at the same time is also so complicated that a lifelong study on prayer still fails to give us total understanding of what it is or how it works.

This little book is a primer to get us started with some basics on prayer. Our intention is to start with the easiest of prayers, "*God, be merciful to me, the sinner! (Luke 18:13)*" and conclude the book understanding what a life of prayer can mean for Christians as we walk our lives daily before God.

> *I have called upon You, for You will answer me, O God;*
> *Incline Your ear to me, hear my speech.*
> *(Psalm 17:6)*

To Be Heard In Prayer

The first book in this series, *Josiah's Sanctification*[1], taught us the importance of being sanctified and how we can achieve being like Christ in our Christian walk. Sanctification generally precedes our prayers because without sanctification in the life of a believer, God will not hear us:

> *If I regard wickedness in my heart,*
> *The Lord will not hear.*
> *(Psalm 66:18)*

To understand this concept completely, we need to start with a few principles. First, a person who is not yet a Christian who calls on the name of the Lord will be saved:

> *And it will come about that whoever calls on the*
> *name of the LORD will be delivered*
> *(Joel 2:32; Acts 2:21, Romans 10:13)*

This initial prayer, said with faith and belief, ushers us into the kingdom of heaven. Without this prayer, we cannot be saved, and a sinner who has just confessed their need for Christ is hardly sanctified. Like the thief on the cross crucified with our Lord, once we see the depth of our sin and call on Jesus for salvation, such a prayer saves us:

> One of the criminals who were hanged there was hurling abuse at Him, saying, "Are You not the Christ? Save Yourself and us!" But the other answered, and rebuking him said, "Do you not even fear God, since you are under the same sentence of condemnation? And we indeed are suffering justly, for we are receiving what we deserve for our deeds; but this man has done nothing wrong." And he was saying, "Jesus, remember me when You come in Your kingdom!" And He said to him, "Truly I say to you, today you shall be with Me in Paradise (Luke 23:39-43)."

Once we are saved, we have the command from Christ to begin walking with God. We will not discuss that matter in great detail here since that was the thesis of the first book in this series. When we accept the title of 'Christian' we are thus commanded to walk in a manner worthy of His name:

> So this I say, and affirm together with the Lord, that you walk no longer just as the Gentiles also walk, in the futility of their mind (Ephesians 4:17).

If we are constantly living our life outside His will and teaching, we are not even doing the simple first things He calls us to do. Our calls on Him will go unanswered:

> *Then they will call on me, but I will not answer;*
> *They will seek me diligently but they will not find me,*
> *Because they hated knowledge*
> *And did not choose the fear of the LORD.*
> *(Proverbs 1:28-29)*

The important first learning objective to be heard in prayer is to be sanctified by studying the Scriptures and hiding the Word in our hearts that we may not sin against God (*Psalm 119:11*).

Prayer, Change, Us, And God

As we embark on our study of prayer, we need to ask to what end we are praying. Can our prayers change the path of an immutable God? Are our prayers more about bringing our will in alignment with His will? If God knows all things already, why are we praying at all? I hope to answer these questions now.

One of the attributes of God described in theology is His *immutability*. This word literally means unchangeable, or without variance. The doctrine means God is the same yesterday, today, and forever as extracted from *Hebrews 13:8* among other verses in the Bible. The question before us now is whether our prayers can change an unchangeable God.

This difficult answer is not entirely settled in the world of Christendom, but I will do my best to answer the questions based on my understanding after weighing many arguments on the subject from many different theologians.

First, God is never informed of anything we need, even as we pray (*1 John 3:20*). There is no thing in this world He does not already know, yet He still commands us to come to Him in prayer (*Ephesians 6:18*), even when we do not know how to pray in a given situation (*Romans 8:26*). We can only assume He calls for us to pray as a test. Are we going to be obedient to bring even the most difficult tasks to His attention in prayer?

C.S. Lewis writes an illustrative scene about prayer and God's sovereignty in *The Magician's Nephew*[2].

Digger, Polly, and Fledge stop to camp on the way to the garden to pluck the fruit at Aslan's request. As they stop, Digger and Polly announced their hunger and say they should have asked Aslan for food to take on the journey. Digger says the great lion should have known they needed food, but Fledge rebukes him saying that Aslan is probably a person who likes to be asked for things, even though he already knows what is needed.

God knows what we need but when we withhold the request, he withholds our needs as a generality. This means that somewhere in the mystery of God's sovereignty He makes ready what we need and delivers it upon our requests. I do not think God's mind is changed, even in the situation we will see later when Hezekiah receives a different answer from God about his illness before and after his prayers.

Taken together, we cannot change God's mind, but somewhere in the mystery of our faith we are given our desires that are in alignment with His will. This is what our prayer is for God: He wants us to ask for what He already knows we need, as a test of our obedience. **So our prayers do not change God, they**

test us if we respond to His commands. Or put another way, prayer is about changing us by bringing our desires into alignment with God's will.

Prayer And Worship

Our ultimate purpose is to worship God. We worship Him when we study our Scriptures, when we attend a church service or another gathering of believers to study the Word, when we sing praises, and as it relates to this book, we worship God when we pray.

Worship is to have fellowship with God, and we have no better direct fellowship than when we talk to Him. Prayer is a two way conversation, not just us listing off a lot of requests to make our lives better and happier as if we were perched on Santa's lap awaiting the promises of Christmas. Instead, prayer is spending time with God, communicating, conversing, and waiting. While we do not generally audibly hear Him speaking back to us, we sense His providence in our life, and we feel His love as we continue on, knowing He has heard us.

When we approach prayer as a part of our worship, we are less concerned with our own desires and more concerned in spending time with Him. Our prayers can take the form of supplication, which is what we would call 'prayer requests', but there is a lot more to having a divine conversation than Him giving us things. In fact, when we think of our own personal, earthly desires for our worldly pleasures, that is the type of prayer He will not answer:

You ask and do not receive, because you ask with wrong motives, so that you may spend it on your pleasures (James 4:3).

To contrast this, worship occurs when we draw near to Him and seek to please God in our life. The natural consequence of fellowship is exultation in the glory of God:

Draw near to God and He will draw near to you. Cleanse your hands, you sinners; and purify your hearts, you double-minded. Be miserable and mourn and weep; let your laughter be turned into mourning and your joy to gloom. Humble yourselves in the presence of the Lord, and He will exalt you (James 4:8-10).

When we approach the throne of God with a humble heart, seeking to please Him and to talk with Him, He exalts us beyond what we could imagine. To experience such closeness, **start viewing prayer as a time to spend with God in conversation rather than going to Him to get your needs met.**

Be Humble In Prayer

The final learning objective is to be humble in our prayers. It is very clear from many scriptures that pride is an offense to God, for even Satan was banished from heaven for being prideful in his attempt to usurp God (*Isaiah 14:12-15*).

Perhaps the best scripture about our need for being humble comes from the parable Jesus tells regarding the Pharisee and a tax collector praying in the temple (*Luke 18:10-14*):

> *Two men went up into the temple to pray, one a Pharisee and the other a tax collector. The Pharisee stood and was praying this to himself: 'God, I thank You that I am not like other people: swindlers, unjust, adulterers, or even like this tax collector. I fast twice a week; I pay tithes of all that I get.' But the tax collector, standing some distance away, was*

even unwilling to lift up his eyes to heaven, but was beating his breast, saying, 'God, be merciful to me, the sinner!' I tell you, this man went to his house justified rather than the other; for everyone who exalts himself will be humbled, but he who humbles himself will be exalted.

The ultimate point of this parable is we can have everything looking correct in our life in terms of perfect tithing, perfect church attendance, and all the other things that come with being a 'good Christian person' but if we do not approach God with the humility He asks us for, He looks away (*Matthew 23:12*).

The humility required in prayer is akin to the love required in the church service (*1 Corinthians 13:3*). While we may have everything the world looks at in line with the Bible, God is the one who truly knows our heart, **so our chief objective is to be humble as we approach the throne of God**.

Prayer And The Word

We have already mentioned that prayer to receive our own desires is not honored by God, but can we ask for absolutely anything? Jesus suggests we can:

Truly I say to you, if you have faith and do not doubt, you will not only do what was done to the fig tree, but even if you say to this mountain, 'Be taken up and cast into the sea,' it will happen. And all things you ask in prayer, believing, you will receive (Matthew 21:21-22).

Some have taken this verse to justify many of the faulty theologies including the health and wealth, name it and claim it gospels, but this expression is one of Jesus's oft-used hyperbole. This particular section was dealing with unity. An examination of prayer shows us that we cannot move our local mountain with prayers, and that was not the point Jesus was making. His point was one of faith and obedience to the Word. In other words, when we pray, we must take out prayers to God based on what He has promised in His Word. Thus, **we must pray the Word back to God and prepare our prayers as those which are aligned with God's promises.**

Chapter Summary

Our learning objectives for this chapter are to **start with sanctification before we expect to have a deep prayer life with God.** This means we are working hard to live for God before we desire to have Him give us things we ask for. Next, to understand why we pray, we need to consider that prayer is not about us getting what we want for our worldly pleasures, **it is about bringing our will into alignment with God's will.** Third, we must approach prayer seeking to honor God in worship. Such prayer is not our one-sided begging of God, so consider prayer as **both a conversation and a means of worship.** Next, **God must be approached with a humble heart.** If we place our pride behind us and seek God fully, we will be heard in prayer, God will draw near to us, and we will receive His blessing. And finally, **our prayers should reflect the Word God has given us in the Bible.** Seeking things He has not promised is generally outside of His will.

2
Hezekiah: A Time of Faith

Then my enemy will see,
And shame will cover her who said to me,
"Where is the Lord your God?"
My eyes will look on her;
At that time she will be trampled down
Like mire of the streets.
It will be a day for building your walls.
On that day will your boundary be extended.
It will be a day when they will come to you
From Assyria and the cities of Egypt,
From Egypt even to the Euphrates,
Even from sea to sea and mountain to mountain.
And the earth will become desolate
because of her inhabitants,
On account of the fruit of their deeds.
(Micah 7:10-13)

ezekiah ruled Judah for twenty years alone, but he was also a co-regent king, sharing the kingdom at times with both his father (Ahaz, 732 – 715 BC) and his son (Manasseh, 695 – 686 BC). Ahaz was a truly wicked king who worshiped gods asking for child sacrifice, even adopting the religious rituals from various surrounding nations. But Hezekiah's son, Manasseh, was actually considered the most wicked king in the entire history of the southern territory.

Hezekiah came to power during the most difficult times in Judean history. Shortly after his birth, his wicked father, Ahaz, offered him as a burnt offering to Moloch (*2 Chronicles 28:3*), but Jewish history records his mother, Abi, saved him by rubbing him in salamander oil[3]. Such a treatment supposedly saved his life, though he may have been physically scarred by such an event.

The same traditions also hold that Ahaz banned the God-ordained means of worship preventing the open teaching of the Mosaic law causing Isaiah to teach mostly in secret. Such disdain for God likely caused Hezekiah to seek out and learn about the only deity his father so passionately rejected.

As a final confirmation during his early co-regency, he watched the Israelite nation be carried off into exile by the same Assyrian army from which his father sought protection (*2 Chronicles 28:16*). Being raised in a land so hostile to his heritage left him marked in body and soul, so he truly sought out the God of his forefathers to seek counsel on how to run his kingdom. Hezekiah's faithfulness to the Mosaic Law gave his kingdom a full revival including the many blessings promised for following God's decrees (*Deuteronomy 28:1-14*). His earnest desire to seek God also showed him the mighty ways God works in our world.

The Regional Conflict

Hezekiah grew up in the conflict of war. The Assyrian kingdom was growing larger, waging war with the region while a coalition of kings including Syria and Israel (*Isaiah 7:5-6*) wanted to depose Hezekiah's father, Ahaz, and install a king sympathetic to their faction. Ahaz fought back against Syria by joining forces with Assyria helping Tiglath-Pileser (the king of Assyria) to destroy Damascus, the capital of

Syria (*2 Kings 16:9*). Ahaz won that victory, but Tiglath-Pileser would soon after turn away from Ahaz in his bid to conquer Judah next.

When Damascus fell, Assyria controlled Egypt, the Philistines, and Babylon up to the Lydian and Median empires. The only section of land not under their direct control was the tiny sliver of land including the central section of the land promised to Abraham, Isaac, and Jacob. It was during this conflict when Hezekiah became king and co-regent with his father for about 14 years.

Six years after the beginning of Hezekiah's co-regency, Israel was finally invaded by the Assyrians and carried off into exile leaving only the kingdom of Judah as being the only section of land not under Assyrian control (*2 Kings 17:6*). During the early part of Hezekiah's reign, he fought against the Philistines pushing the territory controlled by the Assyrians further south, but finally Sennacherib, the new king of Assyria, came for Judah. Hezekiah responded by first trying to buy off Sennacherib with gold and silver, but when that did not work, he sought the Lord in prayer.

Hezekiah's Prophets

During Hezekiah's reign, three prophets were active to the various local regions. The first, Hosea, preached to the northern kingdom exclusively in a word picture about unfaithfulness (*Hosea 1:2*) and redemption (*Hosea 14:4-7*). He was Israel's final alarm bell sounding in the spiritual wilderness before the Assyrian's came to export the people from the northern kingdom as captives. Hezekiah did not have any apparent interaction with Hosea, but the prophet was preaching during Hezekiah's co-regency with Ahaz.

The next prophet, Micah, was preaching in Judah. His message was one of warning, proclamation, and final redemption. Micah was from Moresheth (*Micah 1:1*) which was about 25 miles southwest of Jerusalem near the Philistine border. He prophecies a final warning for the northern kingdom, but they were carried into exile during the early part of his ministry. His prophecies warned Judah about the sin they were committing (*Micah 1-2*) and how they were being prepared for divine judgment (*Micah 3-5*), and finally, he left embedded in his writing a final hope for the faithful people who did not follow the wicked ways of the rest of the nation (*Micah 6-7*). While Micah did preach to the people of Judah, we do not have any evidence he ever spoke directly to any of the kings in the southern territory.

Isaiah is the most influential prophet in the Old Testament, and he had direct interaction with both Ahaz and Hezekiah. He appeared to be from an important family in Judah because first, he was very highly educated as evidenced by the diversity in the language recorded in his prophecies. He also had regular direct contact with the kings, which was generally characteristic of being from a wealthy or connected family. It was Isaiah whom Hezekiah sought for advice regarding the two most important incidents in his life: the risk of Assyrian conquest and an illness that threatened his life.

Isaiah was a prophet to the southern kingdom, but he also overlapped in messages for the surrounding regions proclaiming judgments for many of the local nations. While his messages for the other nations are merely of judgment (*Isaiah 13-28*), he offers Israel (as the combined nation) hope of delivery from captivity (*Isaiah 40-48*), a temporary restoration of the nation (*Isaiah 43*), and most importantly, the prophecy of the child born of a virgin who would save the world (*Isaiah 7:13-16*)!

While Isaiah did preach regarding the surrounding nations, he mostly preached to Jerusalem. He sought out Ahaz to deliver prophetic messages, but Hezekiah actively sought the prophet to hear from God. The interaction between Isaiah and Hezekiah is so great, we find direct textual overlap of the prophecies in Isaiah and the accounts recorded in 2 Kings (*Isaiah 36-39, 2 Kings 18-20*). Not only is Isaiah among the most important prophets in the Old Testament, but he was also the most important prophet to Hezekiah having shown the king that God rewards obedience to His commands.

Legacy Of His Life

Hezekiah was called the greatest king in Judah after the split of the nations because he was the first king that not only objected to the false worship, but he also actively removed the false worship from the kingdom by destroying the altars (*2 Chronicles 31:1*), and reinstating the true worship as commanded by Moses (*2 Chronicles 29:5-11*). He was also the first king since Solomon to re-institute the required feasts the Israelite nation was commanded to continually observe (*2 Chronicles 30*).

After the reinstatement of the old ways of worship, the king rebelled against Assyria, but we shall see how God intervened in that conflict preserving Hezekiah's rule as a direct answer to the prayers he offered up because of the blasphemous messages Sennacherib uttered toward God and His city.

If the conflict in Hezekiah's life was not already enough, he was struck with an illness. We will discuss the various proposed dates for the king to become ill, but the most probable timeline was during the battle with Assyria. He took ill and was bedridden; he knew it was fatal, so he sought Isaiah who gave him the answer he did not want. Once again, Hezekiah turned to prayer and God answered granting him longer life and victory over his enemies. These two prayers give us a look into how a man raised with war and conflict placed in history between two tyrants, became known the as the greatest king since David.

Chapter Summary

Hezekiah was born to a wicked king at the point in history when God was fulfilling the words to His prophets about the coming wrath for their disobedience. Hezekiah saw first hand the exile of the Northern Kingdom and then that same army marching toward him.

Unlike his father, however, Hezekiah placed his faith in God, not just when times were tough but as an extension of his life. He learned about the evil God was going to bring on His nations because of their disobedience and turned to Isaiah for help. He learned to place his trust in God, being delivered twice by prayer. The next chapter will give us some insight into why Hezekiah's prayers where heard by God Almighty.

3

A Sanctified Reign

Come and let us go up to the mountain of the LORD
And to the house of the God of Jacob,
That He may teach us about His ways
And that we may walk in His paths.
For from Zion will go forth the law,
Even the word of the LORD from Jerusalem.
And He will judge between many peoples
And render decisions for mighty, distant nations.
Then they will hammer their swords into plowshares
And their spears into pruning hooks;
Nation will not lift up sword against nation,
And never again will they train for war.
(Micah 4:2-3)

Hezekiah did not live the wicked life of his forefathers then seek God for help when the going got rough. He started his rule as we all must start our own walk with God: *Sanctification*.

We read in *2 Chronicles 29:3-8*:

In the first year of his reign, in the first month, he opened the doors of the house of the LORD and repaired them. He brought in the priests and the Levites and gathered them into the square on the east. Then he said to them, "Listen to me, O Levites. Consecrate yourselves now, and consecrate the house of the LORD, the God of your fathers, and carry the uncleanness out from the holy place. For our fathers have been unfaithful and have done evil in the sight of the LORD our God, and have forsaken Him and turned their faces away from the dwelling place of the LORD, and have turned their backs. They have also shut the doors of the porch and put out the lamps, and have not burned incense or offered burnt offerings in the holy place to the God of Israel. Therefore the wrath of the LORD was against Judah and Jerusalem, and He has made them an object of terror, of horror, and of hissing, as you see with your own eyes.

At the very beginning of his reign, Hezekiah began cleaning up not only his personal life as other kings had done in their life (*2 Kings 12:2-3, 2 Kings 14:3-4, 2 Kings 15:3-4*), but he also began calling on the people of his kingdom to bring their lives into alignment with God's regulations. From this section, we see him open the doors to the temple, call on the Levites to be consecrated, clean the wicked idols out of the temple, and start burning the incense as was required by the Mosaic Law. His reason was simple: *The wicked acts of the Israelite communities are the reason God is judging His people.* Hezekiah knew the first step to pleasing God is to follow his commands with a humble heart (*Psalm 51:16-17*).

The reforms started during the first year of his co-regency. The Northern Kingdom was still battling with Assyria, and Hezekiah knew from Isaiah that the reason God's chosen people were suffering was that they had turned from His law. So when he cleaned up the temple and re-instituted the Passover, he invited his northern brothers to join in the feasts, but most of them laughed at the king for his celebration (*2 Chronicles 30:10*). Five years after this rejected invitation, the Assyrian army carried the Northern Kingdom into exile.

After the Passover, the people went from town to town in Judah cleansing the land of idols (*2 Chronicles 31:1*), reinstating the tithes (*2 Chronicles 31:4*), and re-establishing the whole Law of Moses (*2 Chronicles*

31:20-21). Hezekiah was preparing the kingdom to once again receive God's blessings as promised for obedience in *Deuteronomy 28:1*:

> *Now it shall be, if you diligently obey the LORD your God, being careful to do all His commandments which I command you today, the LORD your God will set you high above all the nations of the earth.*

The Importance Of Sanctification

Hezekiah understood the first step to open lines of communication with God was to stop the flow of sin in the kingdom. *Psalm 66:18* tells us:

> *If I regard wickedness in my heart,*
> *The Lord will not hear.*

This is not just an Old Testament practice. Jesus reiterates two separate times the importance of being sanctified in passages recorded by John:

> *We know that God does not hear sinners; but if anyone is God-fearing and does His will, He hears him.*
> *(John 9:31)*

> *If you abide in Me, and My words abide in you, ask whatever you wish, and it will be done for you.*
> *(John 15:7)*

As Hezekiah began his reign, his first task was cleaning idol worship out of his country. He was allowing God's Word to abide in him. Likewise, we are called on to live an obedient life before God, which is the doctrine of *Sanctification*, or conforming our life to that of Christ:

For this is the will of God, your sanctification; that is, that you abstain from sexual immorality; that each of you know how to possess his own vessel in sanctification and honor, not in lustful passion, like the Gentiles who do not know God; and that no man transgress and defraud his brother in the matter because the Lord is the avenger in all these things, just as we also told you before and solemnly warned you (1 Thessalonians 4:3-6).

From these verses, we see that if we are treasuring sin of either lust or sordid gain, God may not listen to our prayers. For Hezekiah, the kingdom following Baal and Asherim would fall under divine judgment as prophesied by Hosea, Micah, and Isaiah. This divine judgment came upon their lands and was a warning to future citizens in Israel about the importance of obeying God. The warnings recorded in the Old

Testament prophecies, however, are for us as much as they were for the Hebrew nation.

In modern times, obeying God means we need to turn from our own worldly pleasures and follow Christ. If we become distracted by modern entertainment, for example, to the point we are not spending time in fellowship with God or doing His service, we may find ourselves under divine judgment. Generally speaking, in our western cultures we watch more hours of television than we spend collectively praying, studying the Word, or engaging in Christian service. We spend more money on entertainment than any form of Christian giving. Other people are not pulled away from following Jesus by entertainment but by social media instead. As a whole, social media is generally an addictive time waster for most people[4], and that is precious time better spent on fellowship or learning to put more of God's Word in practice in our lives. Yet a third example is politics. Yes, some of us get so tied up in politics that we forget our task is to learn about Christ, put those teachings into action in our own lives, and then pass that information on to other people as we share the Gospel. Some get so tied up in politics that they forget what our real purpose on this planet is: to make disciples of Jesus Christ! Yes, involvement in these worldly pleasures can have value, but we must not let anything distract us from our real purpose of following Jesus in obedience.

It also comes after we have engaged in services God sees as useful for the world (*Matthew 25:31-46*). The Christian life for us is to do more than go to church on Sunday and then live for our earthly pleasures. Hezekiah knew that, and he ordered his subjects to follow the commands laid out by God.

Though we may see sin in our past, or even now presently in our life, we are not to brood in our own condemnation (*Romans 8:1*). Regardless, we are to work out our salvation by living a life that pleases God so we are not waiting for tragedy to make us turn to Him; let us sanctify our hearts and turn to God now! Let us be Christ's disciples and stand firm against the enemy when he comes to fight against us (*Ephesians 6:10-20*). This is our first step toward having our prayers heard.

41

For a more detailed instruction into what it means to be sanctified, read through the first book of this series, *Josiah's Sanctification.* The book explains the logic and reason for needing sanctification and it covers specific tips to live our lives for Christ, including an action plan by which we can learn to follow God.

Chapter Summary

In this chapter we looked at specific steps Hezekiah took in preparation for walking with God. He removed the idol worship and reinstated the laws handed down by Moses. This sanctification of his reign became important later on when he was battling two major events in his life which will be the focus of the next two chapters.

We can learn from Hezekiah's example that obeying the Scriptures is our first path to being heard by God in prayer. Remove the wicked things from our life and turn wholly back to God. The first principle in having our prayers heard is that **God answers those who are obedient.**

4

The First Prayer

This One will be our peace.
When the Assyrian invades our land,
When he tramples on our citadels,
Then we will raise against him
Seven shepherds and eight leaders of men.
They will shepherd the land of Assyria
with the sword,
The land of Nimrod at its entrances;
And He will deliver us from the Assyrian
When he attacks our land
And when he tramples our territory.
(Micah 5:5-6)

ezekiah became a thorn in Assyria's flesh when he rebelled against the nation by failing to pay tribute and defeating the vassal-state Philistines, pushing down their defenses to the south. In the subsequent years, the Assyrian army conquered all the remaining lands including Hezekiah's northern brothers. But finally, Sennacherib, the new king of Assyria came for him. The army marched against Judah in Hezekiah's fourteenth year as king (701 BC).

Now in the fourteenth year of King Hezekiah, Sennacherib king of Assyria came up against all the fortified cities of Judah and seized them (2 Kings 18:13).

Self-reliance

When trouble comes, all of us seek to fix what ails us by our own hands. Obviously, there is nothing inherently wrong with fixing small things like door-knobs on our own. Such a minor detail is certainly within our scope to manage without consulting God in most cases. But when large trials come upon us, it is best for us to seek God in these matters first. Our modern western life might include news we have been diagnosed with a serious illness or that a child has become gravely injured. We should also consult God while making long term decisions such as marriage or employment. Sometimes it is prudent to seek God on whether a matter should be brought before Him.

In Hezekiah's case, the army which has conquered the rest of the known world was now coming to seize his kingdom. This matter would be best handled by talking to God, particularly since Isaiah, whom was well known to Hezekiah, was preaching about Assyria during his own kingship (*Isaiah 14:24-27*). But rather than seek God first, Hezekiah chose an attempt at placating Assyria with a bribe:

> *Then Hezekiah king of Judah sent to the king of Assyria at Lachish, saying, "I have done wrong. Withdraw from me; whatever you impose on me I will bear." So the king of Assyria required of Hezekiah king of Judah three hundred talents of silver and thirty talents of gold. Hezekiah gave him all the silver which was found in the house of the LORD, and in the treasuries of the king's house. At that time Hezekiah cut off the gold from the doors of the temple of the LORD, and from the doorposts which Hezekiah king of Judah had overlaid, and gave it to the king of Assyria (2 Kings 18:14-16).*

Hezekiah stripped the wealth out of the nation in a feeble attempt to stop a tyrant who had already pillaged all of the other surrounding lands. It was a plan destined to fail if circumstances relied only on his own power to save himself. The only result of this attempted bribe was time wasted which Hezekiah could have spent instead on preparation, but he had fewer resources to use because of the wealth handed off to Sennacherib. In deed, Hezekiah may have paid the largest stupid tax in all history!

We can learn from Hezekiah's blunder here. When we attempt to solve life's large problems by our own power, we set ourselves up for failure and further loss. Hezekiah did not stop Assyria's march against him, and we will not stop the difficulties in our life from marching against us without trusting in God.

But The Lord Directs His Steps

The mind of man plans his way,
But the Lord directs his steps.
(Proverbs 16:9)

There is some conflict in our minds when it comes to trusting in God. Some people will do absolutely nothing, waiting for a miracle to come along to save them from difficult circumstances. This is not the way God works. He wants us to plan, to do what we can, but we need to be earnestly seeking Him while we do it. Our first steps, as we have seen in this book and the prior book in this series, is that we need to be obedient to God, following the directions laid forth in His Word. That means we also need to be regularly reading the Bible and praying.

The second step is to do some action that is in alignment with Scripture. Such action could be building up defenses for the coming storm. In our modern world that means having a savings account to plan for emergencies. We are not expected to have nothing, give everything away, and then wait for a miraculous check to show up so we can pay for emergencies that befall us. We find evidence for planing in many of the proverbs:

> *There is precious treasure and*
> *oil in the dwelling of the wise,*
> *But a foolish man swallows it up.*
> *(Proverbs 21:20)*

In short, we find a summary of this principle by Saint Ignatius:

> Pray as though everything depended on God;
> act as though everything depended on you.

To see this action at work, we turn to *Nehemiah 4:9*:

> *But we prayed to our God, and because of them we set up a guard against them day and night.*

Following this principle, the king saw Sennacherib would not be not stopped in his pursuit of the city so, Hezekiah prepared for the conflict:

> *Now when Hezekiah saw that Sennacherib had come and that he intended to make war on Jerusalem, he decided with his officers and his warriors to cut off the supply of water from the springs which were outside the city, and they helped him. So many people assembled and stopped up all the springs and the stream which flowed through the region, saying, "Why should the kings of Assyria come and find abundant water?" (2 Chronicles 32:2-4)*

But in his preparations, Hezekiah was not relying on his own strength, but in God:

> *Be strong and courageous, do not fear or be dismayed because of the king of Assyria nor because of all the horde that is with him; for the one with us is greater than the one with him. With him is only an arm of flesh, but with us is the LORD our God to help us and to fight our battles (2 Chronicles 32:7-8).*

After Hezekiah failed to seek God and losing resources in the process, he relied on God, sent up prayers, and then prepared for the coming assault. His preparations included cutting off the enemies resources by stopping up the wells and then instructing his soldiers to rely on God and not to respond to the Assyrians.

The Assault On God

As the city closed up in preparation for a siege, the Assyrian general, Rabshakeh, stood at the conduit of the upper pool outside the city and tried to cast fear on the people. This location holds significance as Isaiah had met Ahaz, Hezekiah's father at that very spot to attempt to convince him not to rely on Assyria for aid against Aram and Israel (*Isaiah 7:3-9*)!

Rabshakeh tried to convince the people that no other nation could help them because the Assyrians were so powerful they have conquered everyone else. But then he tried to turn them from their God:

> *But if you say to me, 'We trust in the LORD our God,' is it not He whose high places and whose altars Hezekiah has taken away, and has said to Judah*

> and to Jerusalem, 'You shall worship before this
> altar in Jerusalem' (2 kings 18:22)?

I find this statement very interesting because it has parallels to what many people in our secular world think about the Christian faith. So many people misunderstand what Christianity is that when they attempt to discredit our faith, they do so on false pretenses. Their misconceptions are not deliberate, but simply due to many false faiths whom call themselves 'Christian' but fail to live up to Jesus's teachings.

In this case, Rabshakeh saw Hezekiah tearing down the false idols and alters as removing the people's ability to worship God which would make Him displeased. Since he did not understand what real faith is, he did not see that Hezekiah's reforms actually pleased God. In a similar light, we do not please God by surrounding ourselves with objects of fake worship or participate in events because we are seeking to please Him, but rather, when we turn our heart fully to Him and become obedient.

The insults on their faith, and also on God continued:

But do not listen to Hezekiah when he misleads you, saying, "The LORD will deliver us." Has any one of the gods of the nations delivered his land from the hand of the king of Assyria? Where are the gods of Hamath and Arpad? Where are the gods of Sepharvaim, Hena and Ivvah? Have they delivered Samaria from my hand? Who among all the gods of the lands have delivered their land from my hand, that the LORD should deliver Jerusalem from my hand?' (2 Kings 18:32b-35)"

In this way, the Assyrian general was trying to turn the people away from Hezekiah and God so they could enjoy their own land and produce. The people had to choose whether to obey God and their king (*2 Kings 18:36*) or to be tempted away by the promise of personal satisfaction (*2 Kings 18:31-32*).

Hezekiah did not waver in his faith. He mourned over the words delivered by his messengers and immediately entered the house of the Lord for prayer (*2 Kings 19:1*). While he was praying, he also sent word for Isaiah to hear a message from God:

> *Isaiah said to them, "Thus you shall say to your*
> *master, 'Thus says the LORD, "Do not be afraid*
> *because of the words that you have heard, with*
> *which the servants of the king of Assyria have*
> *blasphemed Me. Behold, I will put a spirit in him so*
> *that he will hear a rumor and return to his own land.*
> *And I will make him fall by the sword in his own*
> *land."' (2 Kings 19:6-7)"*

After Isaiah delivered his message to the king, Rabshakeh returned with a final declaration from Sennacherib written on a scroll:

> *"Thus you shall say to Hezekiah king of Judah, 'Do*
> *not let your God in whom you trust deceive you*
> *saying, "Jerusalem will not be given into the hand of*
> *the king of Assyria." Behold, you have heard what*
> *the kings of Assyria have done to all the lands,*
> *destroying them completely. So will you be spared?*
> *Did the gods of those nations which my fathers*
> *destroyed deliver them, even Gozan and Haran and*
> *Rezeph and the sons of Eden who were in Telassar?*
> *Where is the king of Hamath, the king of Arpad, the*
> *king of the city of Sepharvaim, and of Hena and*
> *Ivvah?' (2 Kings 19:10-13)"*

Once again, Sennacherib has defied God and set himself up as more powerful. He had the military resources to annihilate Hezekiah and no human force could hold him back. It was totally up to God, and Hezekiah knew that.

Hezekiah's Prayer

When Hezekiah was presented the scroll containing the demand of surrender, he took it to God in prayer.

Then Hezekiah took the letter from the hand of the messengers and read it, and he went up to the house of the LORD and spread it out before the LORD. Hezekiah prayed before the LORD and said, "O LORD, the God of Israel, who are enthroned above the cherubim, You are the God, You alone, of all the kingdoms of the earth. You have made heaven and earth. Incline Your ear, O LORD, and hear; open Your eyes, O LORD, and see; and listen to the words of Sennacherib, which he has sent to reproach the living God. Truly, O LORD, the kings of Assyria have devastated the nations and their lands and have cast their gods into the fire, for they were not gods but the work of men's hands, wood and stone. So they have destroyed them. Now, O LORD our God, I pray, deliver us from his hand that all the kingdoms of the earth may know that You alone, O LORD, are God. (2 Kings 19:14-19)"

The king knew he had no recourse against Sennacherib, but that God could fight his battles. He had caused the nation to repent, cast out the false worship, restored the temple and the feasts required by Moses, and now he sought the God of the Universe rather than trying to rely on his own strength or that of his surrounding neighbors. His prayer was one reminding God how he had obeyed His Word, but also reminding God about the things Sennacherib spoke against Him. God hears the prayer and answers through the prophet Isaiah (*2 Kings 19:21-28, Isaiah 37:22-29*). The final declaration God makes on Assyrian king is found in last verse of this prophecy:

> *Because of your raging against Me,*
> *And because your arrogance has come up to My ears,*
> *Therefore I will put My hook in your nose,*
> *And My bridle in your lips,*
> *And I will turn you back by the way which you came.*
> *(2 Kings 19:28)*

God acted on His words: within a couple years, God Himself dealt with the Assyrian army on an appointed day:

> *Then it happened that night that the angel of the LORD went out and struck 185,000 in the camp of*

the Assyrians; and when men rose early in the morning, behold, all of them were dead. So Sennacherib king of Assyria departed and returned home, and lived at Nineveh. It came about as he was worshiping in the house of Nisroch his god, that Adrammelech and Sharezer killed him with the sword; and they escaped into the land of Ararat. And Esarhaddon his son became king in his place (2 Kings 19:35-37).

Just as God had said, the king was turned back to his country by His own hand (*Isaiah 37:29*). Also, as he prophesied in *Isaiah 37:7*, Sennacherib was killed in his own country.

Prayer's Delay

One error we often make as we read through the scriptures is we believe prayer is always answered immediately upon request because that seems to be how the text reads, but the time between when the prayer occurs and when God answers is not always indicated in the text. In this particular prayer for delivery, we do not have an exact time Hezekiah waited between when he prayed and when God actually answered, but it is reasonable from the text that God ended the siege two years after Hezekiah prayed:

> *Then this shall be the sign for you: you will eat this year what grows of itself, in the second year what springs from the same, and in the third year sow, reap, plant vineyards, and eat their fruit (2 Kings 19:29).*

Timing of prayer is an important principle to remember when we are seeking God. He always hears our prayers, but we do not live in a fairy tale world where immediately after we ask for something we instantly get our heart's desire.

Sometimes God delays our prayer because we need to grow in our faith and trust in Him. Sometimes He is waiting for some other event, and other times prayer is delayed because of spiritual warfare (*Daniel 10:10-14*). Whatever the reasons our prayers are delayed, we have the duty to keep trusting in God, as He knows the best times to act and for the best reasons (*John 11:14-15*).

Hezekiah demonstrated faith under persecution. It is not uncommon for us to 'trust' in God when things are going well, but the real question arises when things are not going so well. Do we persevere in our faith trusting God even to the point of death? This is what a true disciple will do. But a false disciple will run away from the faith when persecution comes. That was the message about the seed which fell among shallow ground:

> The one on whom seed was sown on the rocky places, this is the man who hears the word and immediately receives it with joy; yet he has no firm root in himself, but is only temporary, and when affliction or persecution arises because of the word, immediately he falls away (Matthew 13:20-21).

Show yourself a fruitful believer in keeping firm in faith even through great trials.

Chapter Summary

In this chapter we examined how Hezekiah stood against the Assyrian siege by relying on God in prayer. We saw that he started his kingdom on a firm footing by removing the high places and restoring the required worship to the kingdom. When troubles came, he lost ground against Assyria by trying to solve the problem on his own first, but then he placed his complete trust in God. **Our principle in this chapter is to seek God first, not as a last resort, and truly trust Him even when answers do not instantly come in a manner we want.**

5

The Second Prayer

With what shall I come to the Lord
And bow myself before the God on high?
Shall I come to Him with burnt offerings,
With yearling calves?

Does the Lord take delight in thousands of rams,
In ten thousand rivers of oil?
Shall I present my firstborn for my rebellious acts,
The fruit of my body for the sin of my soul?

He has told you, O man, what is good;
And what does the Lord require of you
But to do justice, to love kindness,
And to walk humbly with your God?
(Micah 6:6-8)

he second of Hezekiah's prayers was likely the first one he uttered in historical sequence! When the histories were compiled, they flowed with major events preceding minor ones to keep stories unified rather than breaking everything apart for pure chronology. We find such organization in the history of Hezekiah as the war with surrounding nations was the thesis of Kings and Chronicles, but an important aside in this king's life was his illness:

> In those days Hezekiah became mortally ill. And Isaiah the prophet the son of Amoz came to him and said to him, "Thus says the LORD, 'Set your house in order, for you shall die and not live.' (2 Kings 20:1)"

We do not know the specific details of this illness, but we do know it was some kind of boil (*2 Kings 20:7*). The boil could have come from some infection, or it could have been a miraculous test to elucidate Hezekiah's faithfulness. The only thing we know for sure is that it was fatal, and the king knew it.

Our next question regarding the illness is when it actually occurred. Many people upon simple reading of the text assumes this occurs as a capstone to the king's life: He cleaned up the nation, survived the Assyrians, and then became ill. But that is not the way it happened. The first part of the verse illustrates this is a parallel to the other events: *In those days* the text says.

The Proposed Dates

Historical documents and other parts of the Bible suggest three possible dates for this illness. The first proposed date is between 721-710, which was Berobach-baladan's first period of reign over Babylon. During this period of time, Babylon was under turmoil, being taken and retaken by several kings through conquest. Berobach-baladan (also known as Marduk-ap-la-iddin) was a rare king in this period that not only held the kingship for over a decade, but also reigned in relative peace, rebuilding most of the city and erecting shrines to the various pagan gods including Marduk, the god of his namesake. He is specifically named as the Babylonian king who came to visit Hezekiah after his recovery (*2 Kings 20:12*).

There is no evidence for this date range as the time of Hezekiah's illness, or the visit, other than these being the years this king ruled in the peak of his peace-time reign. Other disqualifies for this date include the timing of Hezekiah's reign. While he was a co-regent with his father Ahaz for a number of years, he only reigned solely for a five year overlap in this date from 715-710 BC. If the visit were before 715, the record would have been attributed to Ahaz instead of Hezekiah, but during this period of time, Hezekiah was busy with purifying the land from false worship and restoring God's commands to the practices of the people (*2 Chronicles 29:5-31*). Also, Hezekiah's heart was more dedicated to God during his early reign, but Hezekiah was prideful during the Babylonian visit (*2 Chronicles 32:25*).

Other biblical evidence for this date not aligning includes information about Hezekiah's early years as king. There was little conflict with Assyria on the account that Babylon was a stronger enemy to Assyria leaving two full kingdoms still governing between Judah and Assyria. Also during this period of time, Assyria was finalizing their conquest on Israel (*2 Kings 18:9-12*) and Hezekiah had already pushed back their southern flank (*2 Kings 18:7-8*). This is all significant because in God's answer to Hezekiah, he says that

Jerusalem will be delivered from Assyria (*2 Kings 20:6b*), but there was presently no conflict between the two kingdoms during Hezekiah's early reign.

Finally, historic records from two separate nations indicate only a single visit between Babylon and Jerusalem and that occurred between 703-701 BC depending on which historical documents are consulted. This visit was apparently an attempt to form an alliance between Hezekiah and Berodach-baladan, who at this time was trying to win back his kingdom from king Sargon of Assyria, who was now reigning in the larger Babylonian territory while Berodach-baladan only ruled over the Babylonian coast.

The second proposed date of the illness is 703 BC. This lines up with the date range of the Babylonian visit to Jerusalem. Many will accept this date as the correct year of the illness because some historians say that Berodach-baladan died in 703, however, both Babylonian and Jewish records dispute that claim placing his death instead between 700 ad 694 BC[5]. The confusion occurred because Berodach-baladan ruled for a second time in 703 BC for nine months, but then retreated to rule over the ocean coast once again when Sennacherib conquered the Babylonian mainland[6].

If we believe the records we have, Berodach-baladan ruled Babylon again between 703-702 BC, but was finally conquered again. All historical records agree he did not die in that battle, but fled to the coast land where he still ruled as king. It is most likely during this period when he sought Hezekiah to form an alliance to retake his homeland from Sennacherib.

The final proposed year for the illness and visit is 701 BC. The strongest evidence for this time frame of illness is prophecy. God said he would give Hezekiah fifteen years more to his life, and he died in 686 BC, exactly 15 years later. But this date also aligns with the prophecy to deliver Jerusalem from Assyria, who was already laying siege to the city in 701 BC. The promise of delivery and the king's extended life were both spoken by Isaiah:

> I will add fifteen years to your life, and I will deliver you and this city from the hand of the king of Assyria; and I will defend this city for My own sake and for My servant David's sake (2 Kings 20:6).

Taken together, I propose 701 BC as the date of the illness and miraculous recovery. This date best matches the historical records and aligns with prophecy recorded in three separate places in the Bible.

The summary of events include the conquest of Babylon by Sennacherib in 702. Berodach-baladan retreats to the coast trying to hold onto his kingship from the east, planning how to regain his kingdom. Sennacherib then lays siege to Jerusalem in late 702 or 701, Hezekiah becomes ill, prays for healing and is answered. The sign of his recovery is a miracle that caused the sun to go backwards (*2 Kings 20:8-11*), an event that was seen around the world. Berodach-baladan then hears the miraculous event was connected to Hezekiah, who is currently under siege by his own enemy, so he sends gifts while seeking an alliance with Hezekiah in 701 BC in an attempt to regain his mainland kingdom back.

Hezekiah's Prayer

When the king knew he was going to die, he sent for Isaiah to inquire of the Lord. The answer told him to get his house in order (*2 Kings 20:1*), but on hearing this, the king's first response was to pray:

> *Then he turned his face to the wall and prayed to the Lord, saying, "Remember now, O Lord, I beseech You, how I have walked before You in truth and with a whole heart and have done what is good in Your sight." And Hezekiah wept bitterly (2 Kings 20:3).*

His prayer focused on his faithfulness to God's Word. He prayed to God to remember his obedience to Moses's commands, how he rid the kingdom of the pagan practices, and how he restored the required feasts and festivals. In other words, he couched his petition on his obedience to the clear commands God gave to the Israelite nation.

This is a great model for prayer. Rather than living like the rest of our culture and then crying out when we get ill, we should learn from Hezekiah in this case. He did not seek out to a God he spent his life ignoring, and in his prayer, he reminded God of his faithfulness.

Likewise, if we are living our life for God, pointing many to Him, obeying the clear commands in scripture, our prayers should reflect that back to God. In this case, in response to Hezekiah's reflection on his life and how he followed God, the Lord answered his prayer immediately:

> *Before Isaiah had gone out of the middle court, the word of the Lord came to him, saying, "Return and say to Hezekiah the leader of My people, 'Thus says the Lord, the God of your father David, "I have heard your prayer, I have seen your tears; behold, I will heal you. On the third day you shall go up to the house of the Lord. I will add fifteen years to your life, and I will deliver you and this city from the hand of the king of Assyria; and I will defend this city for My own sake and for My servant David's sake."' (2 Kings 20:4-6)"*

God promised a miracle accompanied with two distinct promises that we have already explored. First, he promises a specific lifespan the king would enjoy. It is rare for any of us know anything about our lifespan. Of course, no one is promised tomorrow, but in this miraculous work of God, Hezekiah became one of the few people who was promised a tomorrow. Enough tomorrow's for fifteen years in fact! This promise is why we place the date of the illness at 701 BC, because the king died in 686 BC, exactly fifteen years later.

The second promise was one of delivery from the Assyrian army. Also, if we accept the 701 BC date, this aligns with the time when the city was already surrounded and the delegations for delivery had begun. In this case, God promised to fight the battle for the humble king.

Hezekiah asks for a sign that these things will occur. We might causally read the text and think he is disbelieving or ungrateful, but that is not the case. Hezekiah's life stood as a direct contrast to his wicked father. Isaiah, the same prophet speaking to Hezekiah now, confronted his father many years earlier when Ahaz was going out to seek an alliance against his enemies. Prophet met king at the very place Sennacherib's officials now called out their demands of Hezekiah: the end of the conduit of the upper pool (*Isaiah 7:3* compared to *2 kings 18:17*). During this meeting, Isaiah promised delivery and asked Ahaz to give him a sign (*Isaiah 7:10-11*). The wicked king refused to ask for a sign choosing instead to follow his own path. It is in this same light that Hezekiah, being the opposite of his father, did ask for a sign:

Now Hezekiah said to Isaiah, "What will be the sign that the Lord will heal me, and that I shall go up to the house of the Lord the third day?" Isaiah said, "This shall be the sign to you from the Lord, that the Lord will do the thing that He has spoken: shall the shadow go forward ten steps or go back ten steps?" So Hezekiah answered, "It is easy for the shadow to decline ten steps; no, but let the shadow turn backward ten steps." Isaiah the prophet cried to the Lord, and He brought the shadow on the stairway back ten steps by which it had gone down on the stairway of Ahaz (2 Kings 20:8-11).

The sign itself was a miracle. It was a point in history when the rotation of the earth went backwards instead of forwards. This miracle would have been seen on all the earth, and when this sign was connected to the miraculous healing of King Hezekiah at Jerusalem, it is likely the Babylonian emissaries came to him hoping for a miracle to deliver them out of Assyria's bondage as we discussed in the prior section. Whatever the final results, Hezekiah was given the healing and the miracle because he was obedient to God, directed the kingdom back to His laws, and repented in humility. As a result of this prayer, he was delivered from both death and conquest.

Not A Foxhole Convert

A characteristic mark of Hezekiah's prayer is that he did not pray only as a last resort. This significant point is a lesson for all of us as we live our lives with our many challenges. While most of us will probably not find our house surrounded by enemies seeking to do us harm, sudden medical ailments are not uncommon in our day.

When Hezekiah found he was ill, he may have first sought some physicians, though it is not recorded in any of the scriptural accounts of his illness. Even if he had, we should not fault that, and likewise, we should seek some basic medical advice if we find ourselves in similar dire straights. But what is clear is Hezekiah did seek God first in this illness. He prayed to God before trying every other option available, and he clearly thought God could answer his prayer.

What is more important than the obvious lesson here, is Hezekiah did not turn to God as a result of the illness. He was not what we would call a 'fox hole convert'. In other words, Hezekiah did not live his life in the manner he wanted and then upon acquiring a deadly illness, turn to God looking for a miracle. That is sadly how many people approach God in prayer today. Whether or not we profess the name of Christ, we often only seek our own will, our way, and in the process we ignore God and His laws in the ever-present pursuit of happiness and upward mobility. Many of us often only turn to God in times of trouble and then we worry when challenges come. Jesus addressed these worrying types in *Matthew 6:28-33*:

And why are you worried about clothing? Observe how the lilies of the field grow; they do not toil nor do they spin, yet I say to you that not even Solomon in all his glory clothed himself like one of these. But if God so clothes the grass of the field, which is alive today and tomorrow is thrown into the furnace, will He not much more clothe you? You of little faith! Do not worry then, saying, 'What will we eat?' or 'What will we drink?' or 'What will we wear for clothing?' For the Gentiles eagerly seek all these things; for your heavenly Father knows that you need all these things. But seek first His kingdom and His righteousness, and all these things will be added to you.

The requirement Jesus tells us is to seek *first* the kingdom of God and His righteousness. This verse is not the Health and Wealth heresy where we beckon God with certain actions and he gives us health and money. This is specifically about God meeting our needs. It is the same context as God *giving us this day our daily bread* (*Matthew 6:11*).

What we have already seen earlier in this book is that Hezekiah did seek first the kingdom of God and His righteousness as a first priority in his life. The first year of his kingdom saw a reversal of the pagan practices his father established, tore down the altars and idols of false worship and re-instituted the festivals which God commanded through Moses. Hezekiah did not come to those conclusions because of his illness, but his prayer was on the basis that he followed God with all his heart:

Remember now, O Lord, I beseech You, how I have walked before You in truth and with a whole heart and have done what is good in Your sight (2 Kings 20:3).

Because of his obedience to God and his humility before the true prophets, Hezekiah was given the desires of his heart:

Delight yourself in the LORD;
And He will give you the desires of your heart.
(Psalm 37:4)

Like Jesus's teaching, God will give us the desire of our heart, but only if we delight ourselves in Him, which means to trust in the finished work of Christ, repent of our sins, turn our lifestyle toward Him, reach the world with the Gospel and serve mankind with the gifts Christ has given us. When we follow God in those ways, He hears our prayers and gives us the answer we best need. In this case, Hezekiah is granted his request. This is not always the case, as we see Paul, also dedicating his life to God, was answered in his request, but he was not given the answer he initially wanted, but one that was better:

Concerning this I implored the Lord three times that it might leave me. And He has said to me, "My grace is sufficient for you, for power is perfected in weakness." Most gladly, therefore, I will rather

> boast about my weaknesses, so that the power of
> Christ may dwell in me (2 Corinthians 12:8-9).

God does answer and He answers according to our needs. While Hezekiah was granted life and victory, Paul was granted something more: greater power through weakness. God gave each man what he needed according to His good will and council.

Hezekiah started his kingdom following God as the pattern in his life before the major challenges in his kingdom arrived. Likewise, we need to repent of our old pagan and Gentile ways and turn to Christ as the pattern in *our* lives. This means we do not sow wild oats Monday through Saturday and go to church on Sunday praying for a crop failure! Instead, we live every day spending time with Christ, growing our own understanding of Him, conforming our life to his ways, and serving people. Sunday is not our day to think about God, it is one of the seven days a week we think about God. While the rest of our week is about getting into the world with the Gospel, the day we attend services and worship is about fellowship with other believers. This is why it is important to find a church that preaches sermons to Christians and not to unbelievers who find their way into the meeting. The ideal church should welcome anyone who walks in the door, but it should target it's teaching specifically to Christians who use the rest of their week in God's dedicated service.

Chapter Summary

Hezekiah's life modeled a pattern of following God, so when he became ill, he turned to God first seeking what he may do to survive. While the illness appears after the Assyrian siege in the Bible, it likely occurred in the middle of the war around 701 BC. The king fell ill, and he knew it was fatal, so he prayed for deliverance. Because the pattern of his life was to follow God and he humbled himself to His prophecies, Hezekiah was given fifteen more years to live and was further promised deliverance from Sennacherib.

What we can learn most from Hezekiah is that he did not turn to God as a result of tragedy in his life. While most people do actually find God in difficult circumstances, it is not the only way to come to Him.

He was obedient to God from the beginning of his life and always sought through the Word and through Isaiah to do what God commanded him to do. As a result, God answered his request. **If we expect to have our heart's desire answered through our prayers, we need to live a life that is obedient to Christ first.**

6

To Hear a Prayer

But as for me,
I will watch expectantly for the LORD;
I will wait for the God of my salvation.
My God will hear me.
Micah 7:7

Our study of Hezekiah's life has led us to see how he grew up without God, but through Isaiah, he was able to find the Lord. Hezekiah started his kingship bringing the nation back into alignment with God's laws before two major events in his life drove him to plead before God in prayer. In this chapter we will look at the various aspects surrounding Hezekiah and his prayers, and then conclude with a few practical 'how-to' steps of prayer that will help our personal prayer life.

Lessons From Hezekiah

The first lesson we find from Hezekiah is that he was sanctified before he ever called on God during his times of crisis. As we previously mentioned, if we live our lives for ourselves seeking God only when troubles arise, we are reaching out to God as a last resort and not out of our relational love for Him.

Another trait of his was the king's humility in prayer. In both recorded prayers, the king cried before the Lord. He knew God was his only option. When he was able to walk, he prayed before God in the temple (*2 Kings 19:14-19*). During the times of his illness, he was unable to get out of bed, but cried before God nonetheless (*2 Kings 20: 2-3*).

We saw positive and negative motivations in Hezekiah as he sought God in his prayers. In the matter regarding the Assyrian siege, we first saw the king waste time and resources trying to buy off Sennacherib rather than praying first. We learned that, had he prayed before sending off his wealth, he would have known God was going to deliver him. During the illness, we have every indication that he sought God first. Taken together, we understand that we need to bring every request before God as a first response rather than a last resort.

Finally, we see that Hezekiah actually had faith. In the matter over the Assyrian siege, he directed his kingdom to have faith in God and not worry about the large opposing army (*2 Chronicles 32:7-8*). When Hezekiah was ill and Isaiah came back to him to announce God heard his prayers, the king asked for a sign, which was his way of saying he believed God was going to heal him.

So from Hezekiah, we have learned to **be sanctified** in our faith, to **pray before God in humility**, to approach **God as a first reaction**, and to **have faith** in what He will do.

How To Pray

Prayer is a difficult subject on which to elucidate because, on one hand, we run the risk of turning our teaching into a checklist of events that we must do to force God to bend to our will, which is ridiculous. But on the opposite extreme is the risk of asking God for things only to find we are dealing with a sovereign being who acts according to His divine will for His perfect plan. He is not here to be our cosmic vending machine giving us everything we want simply because we ask.

Instead, prayer is a relationship every bit as complicated as we find between us and our spouses or children. Things do not always go the way we want, and we often fail to see the significance of challenges until after we have crossed across the canyon of their consequences. These are the methods we need to remember as we look ahead to this chapter, remembering these are general principles of prayer. Real prayer is not to utter lists of things our heart desires to acquire because it will make us happy.

Precepts

There are many books written about multiple methods and mechanisms of prayer, but this short book will look at just a few methods to keep our focus on God. I will encourage you to look into several of the classics such as D.L. Moody's *Prevailing of Prayer*[7] or Reuben Torrey's *How to Pray*[8].

As we embark, let's consider what Jesus said in the middle of the Sermon on the Mount:

> When you pray, you are not to be like the hypocrites; for they love to stand and pray in the synagogues and on the street corners so that they may be seen by men. Truly I say to you, they have their reward in full (Matthew 6:5).

Our first principle is that we do not pray to be praised by other people for our prowess or elegant words. Such pompous prayers seek only to give us recognition, but Jesus boldly declares such people have their rewards on earth rather than in heaven!

Our regular practice of prayer should be one that is private, between us and God:

> But you, when you pray, go into your inner room, close your door and pray to your Father who is in secret, and your Father who sees what is done in secret will reward you (Matthew 6:6).

To create an atmosphere of prayer, find a place to be alone with God without distraction. This means turning off the phone or leaving it somewhere else.

Find your 'inner room' as Jesus says, meaning a personal and private place to pray. It could also be a specific location such as a certain park or a stump on your favorite walking path. Wherever you find a place free of distraction, use that setting to focus privately on your time with God.

Before we finish this point, let's address public prayer. In the verses above, Jesus was not telling us never to pray in a crowd. We find many instances of group prayer throughout the book of Acts. The distinction here is that we should not be praying in a crowd to be heard by our words or to sound spiritual. There exists a fabulous place for group prayer in our Christian walk, but presently, we are addressing the mechanics of an excellent personal prayer life.

The next tool I find helpful for prayer is a journal. The journal could be a very small, pocket-sized composition book or something larger. Whatever you use, this journal is to keep track of your prayers and the responses you have received regarding those requests. Date your requests, write the prayers and details, leaving room to write down how God answers.

Keep praying for those requests just like the friend who came in the night looking for help (*Luke 11:5-8*).

If we have developed a habit of journaling our prayers, we will find that God really does respond to our requests. Sometimes we receive exactly what we have asked for. Sometimes God withholds His hand from us to teach us something. Other times, God answers in a way we never thought would be possible.

Finally, be consistent with praying. This is another spiritual discipline like Bible study. If we develop the habit of prayer in addition to our plan for Bible study, it will become part of our daily spiritual practices. This counteracts our normal human tendency to pray and study our Bible only when things are not going well.

Consistency is different from persistence. The persistence for a request fades once we have received the response we were looking for, but consistency means we are in a regular practice of praying at our specific time at our specific place, not binding our habit to a specific request, but rather to our devotion for God.

Pray Like This

Jesus' disciples came to Him to learn how to pray. They came to him to ask how to pray because both John the Baptist and the Pharisees were teaching their disciples how to pray, and so they wanted to hear from Jesus how they should lift their requests before God (*Luke 11:1*).

Pray, then, in this way:
Our Father who is in heaven,
Hallowed be Your name.
Your kingdom come.
Your will be done,
On earth as it is in heaven.
Give us this day our daily bread.
And forgive us our debts,
as we also have forgiven our debtors.
And do not lead us into temptation,
but deliver us from evil.
For Yours is the kingdom and
the power and the glory forever. Amen.
(Matthew 6:9-13)

The famous Lord's prayer is not a model to be uttered as a replacement for all prayer, but instead it communicates to his listeners that prayer is about conversation. A proper prayer balances the various aspects of our conversations: praising God, seeking His kingdom, requesting physical needs like food and shelter, seeking strength in our various trials, and generally focusing on heavenly principles.

Dissecting this prayer, illustrates a pattern that is often taught in the acronym called the ACTS prayer:

A – Adoration

C – Confession

T – Thanksgiving

S – Supplication

This is a great tool to think through while praying. In *Adoration*, we are praising God for His attributes and love. *Confession* is repenting of our sins and seeking God's forgiveness daily. *Thanksgiving* is expressing thanks for our blessings, and *Supplication* is asking God for requests we may have.

The point of the Lord's Prayer and the ACTS model is not just to make sure our prayers avoid being rote repetition, which Jesus teaches against (*Matthew*

6:7). The Lord wanted to teach us that prayer is more conversational, being based on our relationship with Him. He started with *Our Father who is in heaven*, and he used the less formal word which we would typically describe is being 'daddy' in our current vernacular. This was very relational. Next He gives the adoration, *Hallowed be Your name*. The adoration continues through the following verse declaring His power of His will over the earth. He ends with confession and supplication as we seek to be forgiven for our sins against Him and other people, but asks for both physical and spiritual needs in the process. This relational prayer is a model for how we should approach God in prayer.

Create Your Personal Plan

If you ask any Christian, they will probably say they want to improve their prayer life. I know I do! I pray this book gives you some insight into one story of prayer that can help us to understand a little more how God works in prayer. With that in mind, we want to end with a brief section highlighting how we can work on having a more robust prayer life.

Be Committed In Your Faith

Commit to God. We cannot expect God to answer our prayers when we do not have a relationship with Him. As we become closer to God through a desire to love Him for who He is, rather than what He can do for us, we will experience more fellowship with Him, we learn more of His will, and we learn how we can please Him in our prayers.

- ❖ Have a desire to please God for who He is

- ❖ Learn what the Bible says and what it means

- ❖ Conform your life to the teachings in the Bible

The Discipline Of Prayer

Develop a habit of prayer. Our spiritual health is compensatory to our participation in the means of grace. That is to say, if we dedicate time to prayer and Bible study we grow closer to God, but if we choose instead to dwell on worldly things, we stay worldly.

- ❖ Schedule time to pray

- ❖ Pray even when you do not feel like it

- ❖ Focus more on God than the things in the world

Find A Place To Pray

Developing a habit of prayer requires **finding a place to pray regularly**. That is not to say we cannot pray in other places as well, but our primary prayer 'closet' should be quiet and free from distractions. It should be a place where we can go and not be disturbed by a phone, a door, or any techno-gadgets. It should also be private and accessible.

- ❖ Find a private place to pray

- ❖ Turn off the phone or leave it elsewhere

- ❖ Avoid distractions

Keep A Record Of Prayer

Have a prayer journal. This could be something large that stays in the prayer location (if your location is at home), or it could be a small composition book that fits in your pocket which you can access any time you want to write down a prayer request or how something was answered. This journal will help you see how God moves in your life in response to your prayers.

- ❖ Have your journal with you when you pray

- ❖ Keep a record of prayers and responses

The Gospel

We have all sinned. In our natural condition, we perform actions displeasing to God. These actions are called sin, and since God cannot be in the presence of sin, we are, by our nature, separated from Him. If we die in this state, we are bound to eternal separation in hell. However, God provided a way out of our deathly state. Jesus Christ, who was fully God and fully man, lived on the earth, was tempted in all ways as we are, and lived a perfect life. Jesus willingly went to a cross and died for our sins so we would be able to be in the presence of God. This sacrifice by Jesus is a free gift that makes us clean before Him.

We take hold of this gift by prayer. We must understand and admit our sinful state, incapable of being able to resist sin. We must acknowledge Jesus has the power to cover our sin. Pray to God to receive Christ's sacrifice on your behalf and you will be cleansed of your sin, both great and small.

If you have prayed to receive Jesus, mind the words in this book. Begin to read the Bible, search out Christian fellowship, and learn what God would teach you. Grow in faith and sanctification, cleanse your heart and submit to God's Word. Welcome to the kingdom.

Bibliography

1. *Josiah's Sanctification*, Thomas Murosky, 2019, Our Walk in Christ Publishing
2. *The Magician's Nephew*, C.S. Lewis, 1955, The Bodley Head
3. Sanhedrin 63b
4. I recognize that some people do use social media for ministry purposes which is a valid use of the time, but in my experience, more people justify the time as ministry when they are merely reposting Christian memes or challenging old friends they have not had real relationship with in years. All of these considerations need weighed.
5. https://www.jewishvirtuallibrary.org/merodach-baladan (Accessed Sept 4, 2019)
6. Chronicle on the Reigns from Nabû-Nasir to Šamaš-šuma-ukin
7. *Prevailing Prayer*, Dwight L Moody, Moody Publishers
8. *How to Pray*, RA Torrey, Work in Public Domain

Scripture Index

Other Books by Thomas Murosky

Josiah's Sanctification

ISBN:

978-1-732569645 (s)

978-1-7325696-5-2 (e)

Lessons Learned From a Lost Book

Testing and Temptations

ISBN:

978-1-7325696-0-7 (s)

978-1-7325696-1-4 (e)

Do you know what it takes to live like Jesus?

I AM not amused

ISBN:

978-1-7325696-2-1 (s)

978-1-7325696-3-8 (e)

Does your entertainment honor God?

About Thomas Murosky

Thomas Murosky has a background in Biological Sciences earning his Bachelors in Biochemistry and his Doctorate in Molecular Toxicology. He taught Chemistry at Bucknell University and Western Wyoming Community College. While as a student and professor, Tom worked in several capacities as a children's and youth worker having served the local CEF board, as a counselor for Christian camps, Awana programs, and other youth outreach including a decade of work in Big Brothers, Big Sisters of America.

Tom stepped aside from teaching and academics to work as a technology consultant to focus more time on writing, blogging, and video production in the area of Christian teaching with an emphasis on discipleship and sanctification. His first book, Testing and Temptations, is about how we are called to transform our lives to be like Christ in the process of Sanctification. His second book, The Art of Shallow Neighboring is parody book calling us to better Christian discernment in the books we read. His third book, I AM Not Amused calls for sober analysis of the media entertainment industry. In addition to these, Tom produces videos on current Christian events and sound theology on OurWalkinChrist on YouTube.

You can find more information and other books Thomas has authored at www.ourwalkinchrist.com. Signup for the newsletter for information on future releases, promotions, and advance reader copies at www.ourwalkinchrist.com/newsletter.